The Community Theatre Actors' Bible

Ten Secrets to Better Acting

for Untrained Actors

by

Lew Holton

BEACH HOOCH BOOKS

Cover design by Tres Holton

1

The quoted passage by Oscar Wilde is from his play, *The Importance of Being Earnest*, first produced in 1895 and published in 1899.

The quoted passage by Mark Dunn is from his play, *Belles*, published by Samuel French, Inc., copyright 1989, 1997 (Revised), and is used with the author's permission.

For Tres and Ashley and Calvin and Reagan.

Special thanks to Bill Bozzone, to Marvin Joe Merck, and to Steve Earnest—friends, mentors, colleagues to whom I turned for trusted and invaluable feedback on this project and from whom I may have borrowed bits of "secrets" over the years. (With apologies to Lowell Ganz and Babaloo Mandel…) If gratefulness were people, I'd be China.

Foreword

The "secrets" contained in this book, admittedly, are not secrets in the purest sense of the word. The techniques, exercises, and tips may be well known to many good directors and old news to trained actors. Community theatres, though, rely on a wealth of generous, talented, and highly motivated actors who may have a wide range of community theatre stage experience, but who have little or no formal training. Those individuals—experienced or brand new—may not be willing to ask questions that they fear might highlight their lack of training. Directors may not wish to appear didactic, but neither do they want to suggest that they are not solidly at the controls. The true value of this book lies in the fact that a community theatre director can hand it to his or her cast members—or simply read it aloud to the cast at one of the first gatherings—and in doing so, establish or reinforce some basics that simply need to be said aloud at the outset of each new production, but which often are not. It provides a foundation upon which a clear and ultimately more productive actor-director relationship may be built, and thus makes it just a little easier to wind up with a show that may *say* "community theatre" on the playbill, but one in which professional standards shine through.

The Community Theatre Actors'

Bible

Ten Secrets to Better Acting

for Untrained Actors

1. Recognize that your character has a life outside of the pages of the script.

2. Trust your director and your fellow cast and crew members.

3. Break down the script into "French scenes."

4. Think of each "French scene" as an *event* in the lives of the characters.

5. Create a memory of each event.

6. Recall the memory each time before you "run your lines."

7. Be "in the moment."

8. Get that book out of your hands.

9. Be open to directorial notes and suggestions.

10. Quit "acting" and have a little fun!

1. **Recognize that your character has a life outside of the pages of the script.**

One of the fundamentals of theatre is that we have to create characters that people want to spend time with, characters that people care about in some way. An audience must at least care enough that they want to see a particular character succeed...or they want to see another character fail...and they must be willing to sit there for ten minutes or two hours in the hope that they will see that happen. As an actor, *you* have to care about your character. If *you* don't care about the character, how can you get the audience to care about your character? By the way, don't confuse "caring" with likeability. One of the most interesting and challenging experiences in

acting is to create a character who is actually
disliked; think of Jack Manningham (the husband) in
Angel Street or Salieri in *Amadeus*. "The way life
works"—our own experience with life—is our
constant touchstone. We care about people that we
know in life—we want to see the ones we like
succeed and the ones we don't like fail—because,
first and foremost, they are *real* to us. They have
actual lives that we know something about, and those
lives have touched our own lives in some way, good
or bad. As an actor, you have to grant your character
a life outside of the pages upon which the character
appears in the script. What did that character do in
the fifteen minutes before we meet her in the script?
In the month before we meet her? In the year before
we meet her? In the ten years before we meet her?

What has been her life, and what is her life now? You have to get to know that character—her best friend and confidante, her husband or boyfriend, her co-workers, her likes and dislikes, her *life*. How *well* must you get to know your character? There are all sorts of opinions volleyed back and forth about that, but here is a pretty good rule of thumb: You should know your character about as well as you know one of your good friends. Do you know *everything* about your good friends? No. Do you know them as well as you know *yourself*? No. But you do know them—you know about their lives—pretty darn well. You could probably sit down and tell a stranger enough about some event in the life of a good friend of yours that the stranger would, first, accept that your friend is *real*, and may even become interested

9

enough to want to sit there and hear how the event in your friend's life turned out. If it is real to you, then you can make it real for someone else. When it comes to your friend's life, you know details, you know specifics. Discover those same details about your character's life. For example, what magazines would your character pick out at an airport bookstore, or where did your character experience his or her first kiss? Once you begin to fill in the blanks of your character's life, then the character can become *real* to you, so that you can make the character real for others.

An artist—any artist—must be vulnerable. To be vulnerable is to be willing to show perfect strangers—or perhaps even scarier, people we may know—the faces and the emotions that we typically guard most closely—not just laughter or anger—laughter and anger are cheap; they cost us nothing in terms of vulnerability—but fears and tears, the ones we don't want most people to see. And fears and tears are rooted in the details of real lives. As we figure out the details of our characters' lives, as they become real to us, we also figure out the sources of their fears and tears, and as we take on those characters' lives, their fears and tears become our own. Of course, we must be willing to share them with the audience. That's the deal. It is the price we pay, as actors, for the extraordinary gift of being allowed to step out of our own lives and into someone else's.

Don't just learn your lines; learn *from* your lines. Look at things your character says, as well as things other characters say *about* your character. These things should *prompt* you to fill in the blanks of your character's life outside the pages of the script. Here is an example of how that works, from Mark Dunn's play, *Belles*, which features six characters who are sisters. One of the sisters, Dust, "capsulizes" one of her dreams—one involving St. Thomas Aquinas, Emily Dickinson, and Buddy Hackett—to her sister, Peggy. She says:

"Anyway, they were all dressed up as geisha girls, pouring each other tea, and singing (*She sings.*) 'Three Little Maids from School.'"

What does this line tell us about Dust's *life*? First— she knows who St. Thomas Aquinas is and how odd it is that he would appear in this particular sequence of her dream. The same for Emily Dickinson and

Buddy Hackett. Second—it tells us that she knows the tune, "Three Little Maids from School." She knows it well enough to sing it. Where does the tune come from? It comes, of course, from Gilbert and Sullivan's *The Mikado*. How does *she* know the tune? Has she seen the operetta so often that she has learned the song? Or…did she perform the song at some time herself…perhaps as part of the cast of a high school production of *The Mikado*? If so, did Peggy come to see her perform the piece? Did her other sisters? Dust is perfectly comfortable making the reference when she is talking to Peggy, so we have to assume that it is a reference that the two of them share in some way. Rather than performing the song as part of a high school production, could this be something that Dust and Peggy used to perform

13

together when they were much younger? If so, which of the other sisters got to be the third "little maid from school" when they performed the song? Which sisters were *not* allowed to be the third little maid? This is only one small example. Look at the things that your character says and see what those lines tell you—*not* about what's going on in the play—but about that character's life *outside* the play.

One of the keys to building a life for your character outside the pages of the script is to put a *face* on each of the people in your character's life, on each of the people mentioned in the script that your character would know—including not just the characters he or she interacts with on stage, but the ones who people his or her life outside the pages of the script—the "backstory" folks, if you will. Where will you *get* all of those faces? You could try to make them up. That's difficult. It's much more practical to borrow them. Use the faces of acquaintances—though probably not best friends— and family—though probably not *close* family— cousins, aunts, uncles. Borrow the faces of people from TV and the movies. *Find* the faces you can use and put them on the people in your character's life. Again, these people have to become real to you before you can begin to make them real for others, and the first step to making someone *real*, for many of us, is to be able to *see* that person's face—to visualize it when we talk about him or her.

The two main ingredients in good acting may well be, first, the ability and the willingness to discover what a character's life has been up until that point when we meet that character in this script, and second, to make what is happening in a particular scene a real event that is part of that character's life as a whole. So—step one—get to know your character like you get to know a new friend.

2. **Trust your director and your fellow cast and crew members.**

A theatrical production has a voracious appetite for the time and energies of the people caught up in its web. Unfortunately, even all of the hard work that you can cram into all of your waking hours still cannot guarantee success if it is not properly focused. Think of it this way: If you and a team of your friends get together and decide to drill for oil, you could expend an awful lot of time and energy and hard work and wind up with little to show for it except a bunch of holes in the ground...*unless* you brought in someone with the know-how to point out *where* and *how* to concentrate all of that effort, and even then only if the team is willing to trust the advice of that person that they have brought in to *direct* their efforts. There certainly may be other richly experienced players connected with a theatrical production, but typically a director brings a wealth of experience to a production. Tap into that experience. Once you've signed on for the journey that a play production always is, you will find it a much smoother voyage if you accept at the outset that the director is the captain of that particular ship. While a good director is usually receptive to the ideas and suggestions of his or her cast and crew, the final decision is the director's. Leave the directing to the director. Good directors are often our best "acting teachers" because they prompt us to explore and to discover new and different possibilities within our acting that we wouldn't have tried on our own. The director can see you on the stage; you cannot see yourself. A good director has a *vision* for the particular play that he or she is directing. When we see a really successful production of a play, it is usually because the members of the cast and crew have done their individual parts to help make that vision a reality. Often, a director, necessarily, has divided loyalties. He must be true to his cast. He must be true to the script, in terms of the playwright's words and intentions. He must be true to the theatre's mission and its role in the community. And even as he tries to be attentive to all of those elements, he must be as true as possible to his own vision of the play. As a member of the cast, however, your loyalties are first and foremost to each other. You must come together as an acting company. You have to be there for each other, because when it all comes together, and the house

lights go down and the stage lights come up, and you

walk out there on that stage, the director is not going

to be out there on the stage. The playwright is not

going to be out there on the stage. The theatre

management or members of the theatre's board of

directors are not going to be out there on the stage.

You and your fellow actors are going to be out there,

and who you will have to rely on and to turn to is

each other. The director's job is to prepare you for

that—to make sure that you are as competent and

comfortable and confident as possible in what you

are walking out there on that stage with. Putting on

a play is a leap of faith, so *have* faith…in your

director…in the crew who are providing the lighting,

sound, props, and all of the other behind-the-scenes

magic…and in each other.

3. **Break down the script into
"French scenes."**

What is a "French scene"? A French scene does not necessarily coincide with numbered scenes in a play. A new French scene occurs whenever the acting dynamics of a scene change because one or more of the characters in a scene leave the scene or because one or more new characters join the scene. For example, Act III, Scene 3 of *Othello* can be said to contain six French scenes. The scene begins with Desdemona, Cassio, and Emilia talking. About thirty lines later, Othello and Iago enter and Cassio exits; we have a new set of dynamics and thus a new French scene. Approximately fifty lines later, Desdemona and Emilia exit the scene, leaving Othello and Iago alone. That creates a third French scene—one in which Iago plants the seed of doubt about Desdemona's fidelity. Some two hundred lines later, Iago exits, and Desdemona and Emilia re-enter for a short fourth French scene. When Desdemona loses the handkerchief and she and Othello leave, we have yet another French scene in which Iago re-enters and talks with Emilia. Finally, Emilia exits, Othello re-enters, and we have the sixth and final French scene within Act III, Scene 3. Breaking the play down into French scenes makes for small bites. Sometimes the idea of taking on an entire full-length play and learning all of those lines can be intimidating. The idea of taking on a scene of only thirty or even a hundred lines is much less daunting. Try it; you'll like it.

4. **Think of each "French scene" as an *event* in the lives of the characters.**

Most often *you* don't have to worry about finding the French scenes; the director will do that for you. Breaking the play down into French scenes not only makes it more manageable, in terms of actors learning lines, but it also allows the director to work one short scene, then another and another, and so on. Good directors have said that they prefer to think of themselves as *scene* directors, rather than *play* directors, because good scenes make for good plays. By concentrating on one scene at a time, we are also establishing and constantly reinforcing the value of thinking of the play in terms of a *series of events*— each event a "moment" within which the actor can immerse himself or herself as his or her character and can internalize that event. If we have granted a character a life outside the pages of the play, then when we come as actors to a short scene involving that character, we can think of that scene as an actual event in the life of that character. If we have made the character *real*, then the events in that character's life become real. They become as real as the events in our own lives.

5. **Create a memory of each event.**

We remember events in our own lives. We don't need to make a conscious effort to remember them; we internalize them because we perceive them to be *real*. We create memories of events, both special and mundane. We remember what we and others who were part of that event in our lives did and said. Often, we can recount entire conversations, *not* because we took the time to memorize the "lines"—the things that we and others said—but because we naturally created a memory of the event. Think about the last time you went to dinner with a friend or the last time you visited with your mom. If you can remember details of an event in your life that happened last year or even last night, including perhaps conversations that took place during that

26

event, then you have all of the working tools for learning a scene. The key, then, is to think of a scene as an event in your character's life and, as you walk through or even just read and visualize a scene, to *create a memory of that event*...exactly as you do for events in your own life. Once you have created a memory of the event, you never have to worry about being "lost" in a scene, even if, Heaven forbid, you were to "lose" a line, because you *know what happens* during that event in the character's life. You naturally remember it just like you naturally remember what happened in your own life yesterday.

6. **Recall the memory each time before you "run your lines."**

How can you tell if that create-a-memory process is working? Here is an exercise. One of the details of your character's life that you should know is who her best friend or "confidante" *outside the play* is. Make sure she has such a person in her life—someone to whom that character can go to and can talk to about just about anything. Notice: that confidante should be someone who is *not* a character that *your* character interacts with in the play, because your character needs to feel free to talk to this confidante about each and every other character that she interacts with in the play. Once you start working on a scene—walking through it, even while still doing it book-in-hand—and then you go home to start trying

28

to learn your lines for that scene, to run your lines with whomever you get with to do that, *begin* by getting into character—then *before* you work on the first line—*tell* that person about the event—about what you remember of the event. Tell that person about it, as if that person were your character's confidante. Tell that person what happened in the scene, as if recounting an event that happened *to you* a little while earlier (which it *did* since you *were* that character then). If you remember parts of the conversation that took place during the event, recount that, as well—even if they are not the exact lines that are on the page. Do this *every* time you begin to run lines. Each time you work on a scene, the details of that "event" will become more and more internalized, just like with repetitive events in

29

your own life. Therefore, each time you recount the memory of that event to whomever you are running lines with—*before* you start running those lines— your recollection of that event should become more and more detailed, including the details of what was *said* during that event, i.e., "the lines."

7. **Be "in the moment."**

What does it mean, to be *in the moment*? It simply means that you are *there*, present, an active participant in a real event going on around you. The key, again, is to enter into the event—the scene—as a *real event*. A play is dialogue-driven. It largely turns on conversations that the audience gets to eavesdrop on. As participants in a real conversation, we *listen* to what the other person is saying. What we say is a *response* to what we have just heard someone say to us. Being *in the moment*, then, is turning a series of "lines" into an actual conversation that involves listening and responding. It is also about reacting to what is going on around us—to what is said and done, to what we hear and see—just as we do in real life. The old cliché about acting

31

being reacting is very much rooted in the truth.

Good acting is the appearance that no acting at all is going on, and a genuine response to what is going on around us within an event is *not* acting; it is *re*acting. As long as we are present and attentive and reactive, we are *in the moment*. And that is exactly where we must be for a scene to truly work.

8. **Get that book out of your hands.**

Learn your lines. The lines are a gift from the playwright to the actor. If you want ultimately to feel liberated as an actor, learn your lines…word for word.   There are actors out there—and they run the gamut from freshest amateur to seasoned pro— whose approach to lines is this: "I'll say something like this…and then you say something like that…and so on and so on." Never mind that they are slighting the playwright; they don't realize what a disservice they are doing to themselves, to their fellow actors on stage with them, and to the overall performance. In the same way that you can't be *in the moment* if you're somewhere else searching for your lines, you can't be *in the moment* on stage if you're busy constantly re-writing what it is that you're about to say. And—once an actor *does* come up with a re-written line that is "something like" what the playwright intended—most of the time the actor who is on the receiving end of that "something like" line is thrust into the position of having to re-write his or her line to make it fit, and thus...*that* actor is taken out of the moment. Take, for example, an exchange as simple as this one, from Oscar Wilde's play, *The Importance of Being Earnest*:

> **Jack:** But you don't really mean to say that you couldn't love me if my name wasn't Ernest?
>
> **Gwendolen:** But your name is Ernest.
>
> **Jack:** Yes, I know it is. But supposing it was something else? Do you mean to say you couldn't love me then?

If the actress playing Gwendolen says "something like" her line, and it comes out, "Are you saying it's not Ernest?" or "But I love the name Ernest," Jack's next line no longer makes sense as a response. So, the actor playing Jack has to stop being Jack for a moment—has to step out of the moment, do a quick re-write, and then step back into the scene with his own hastily assembled "something like" line, "I'm not saying that my name is *not* Ernest; I'm just saying suppose it was something else. Do you mean to say you couldn't love me then?"—in order to get back on track. The scene has suffered because neither actor was fully *in the moment*. Each was briefly "somewhere else," re-writing his or her lines. If that happens throughout the play, those moments add up, and the entire play suffers. Once the actors honestly commit to the lines—*as* they were written—word for word—then the actors don't have to worry about what they *or* their fellow actors in the scene are going to say, and they are *free* to be *in the moment*—to truly make the scene real, to make it come to life.

9. **Be open to directorial notes and suggestions.**

Believe this: Notes and suggestions from a director are not personal attacks on you or your efforts or your choices. Hurt feelings and disharmony are counterproductive to the team effort required to make a play succeed. No director in his or her right mind wants to put on a bad play. If that premise rings true for you at all, it only makes sense to believe that the director's notes and suggestions are intended to make the play as good as it can be. Part of making the play as good as it can be is making *you* as good as you can be, since you are a component of the play. If we lose sight of that truism, even the simplest directorial notes can become needlessly frustrating and contentious.

37

Take, for example, this exchange between actor and director that virtually every community theatre playhouse has witnessed.

> **ACTOR.** Yadda-yadda-yadda.
>
> **DIRECTOR.** Louder! Louder!
>
> **ACTOR.** I feel like I'm shouting now!
>
> **DIRECTOR.** Don't yell; pro*ject!*
>
> **ACTOR.** I'm trying; I'm trying. It doesn't feel *natural.*

Edward Albee once said, "A play is a *heard* thing." He was talking about the craft of playwriting, but it is an observation that stage actors would do well to recognize and remember. One of the things we do in life to try to succeed is to emulate what we believe to be successful ways of doing things that we observe in other people. For many newer community theatre actors, their most common—sometimes their *only*—frame of reference for "how to act" comes from watching screen actors. Unfortunately, as a result, their line delivery is calibrated for a camera and a boom microphone situated a few feet in front of them, rather than for the patron who is seated in the last row at the back of the theatre. The truth is that it *doesn't* feel natural to a newer actor, and it's not what she has seen (and heard) her favorite *screen* actor do. The directorial note, "Louder! Louder!" just feels stranger and stranger and less and less like "acting." And textbook explanations of "using the diaphragm" and "ha ha ha" exercises are rarely a satisfactory solution. To truly "get it," an actor needs somehow to experience her stage conversation both as an actor and as an audience member. How can we make *that* happen? Try this. Take a scene

between two actors in which they are *not* shouting,

but are talking normally, easily, even intimately.

Have one actor assume her normal place on stage.

Have the other actor stand in the last row of the

theatre. Now…play the scene. The actors will

immediately and naturally realize when they cannot

hear each other. Play the scene over and over until

the actors find the volume level they need to play

that scene effectively. The thing to keep in mind,

though, is that, with or without such exercises to

illustrate the point, the original directorial note,

"Louder! Louder!" was offered *only* to help the actor

improve her performance and the overall play.

Remember, it's called a *play* for a reason. It

centers around *playing*: imagining, exploring, trying

new things. Directors' notes and suggestions are rooted in that rich, fertile, "try this" soil. Take notes and suggestions in that spirit and see what happens. If a directorial suggestion doesn't work—if it does *not* help make the play as good as it can be—you can rest assured that a competent and conscientious director will yank it and try something else that works better, that makes you look better, and that makes the play better.

10. **Quit "acting" and have a little   fun!**

Putting on a play is many things to many people. It

is art. It is culture. It is entertainment. It can be

educational. But…among those many things—and

pretty high on the list—is the fact that it ought to be

fun. It should be an enjoyable experience. If it isn't,

why are you doing it? Remember—your energy

level affects the audience's energy level. If *you* are

in the moment, you can pull that audience right into

the moment, as well. If the scene is a *real event* to

you, it is more likely to become *real* for the

audience. If *you* are having fun, the audience is

more likely to have fun. Fun is contagious. The

audience *wants* to enjoy themselves; they *want* to be

entertained; that's why they've come. They are

already receptive. Take that receptiveness and run

with it. Whether your character is making them laugh out loud or is breaking their hearts, *enjoy* being in that moment with them. *Fun* refers to that which is playful or that causes enjoyment. The reason everyone has gathered—on both sides of the footlights—is for a *play*. Quit "acting" and...*play* with *them*.

LEW HOLTON is an award-winning
playwright, an actor, a director, and a teacher.
His plays have been produced in New York and
throughout the wider theatre world.

He has acted professionally in New York and in
regional theatre, and he has appeared in
dozens of community theatre productions.

His teaching *curriculum vitæ* lists Long Island
University, Clemson University, and Coastal
Carolina University. He resides now in the
coastal community of Murrells Inlet, SC.